PATRIOTISM IN AMERICA: IS IT CHANGING?

PATRIOTISM IN AMERICA: IS IT CHANGING?

America is traditionally a very patriotic nation. History shows that any time this nation was threatened its people never failed to rally around the flag and band together to support efforts to repel the perceived enemy. The most contemporary example of this occurred after September 11, 2001 when the world trade center and the Pentagon were attacked by terrorists. Americans, immediately energized by patriotism, rallied around the nation and demanded retaliation. Now we are conducting operations in both Iraq and Afghanistan.

So is patriotism a dangerous attribute? Some might say that the example above is proof of why patriotism should not be considered a virtue. After all it was love of country and wanting to protect her that brought us to conflict. Add to this a world increasingly influenced by globalization and a demand for tolerance and the motivation of the patriot such as that described above becomes potentially detrimental to a country's ability to successfully operate in a global society.   Patriotism is love of country. This love and what one is willing to do to exercise it have caused some to debate the value of the trait. As the world becomes more influenced by the impact of globalization and the demand for tolerance the debate brings to question the motivation of the patriot and how this motivation impacts a country's ability to successfully operate in a global society. The question I will address is how this impacts American patriotism and is it changing? I will discuss the challenges faced by the American patriot and show how the motivation behind their patriotism has basically remained the same. I will follow with a discussion on the differing views of patriotism which challenge the patriot, discuss the guiding principles that have enabled the American patriot to endure through some of the nation's most challenging times, discuss how patriotism is exercised, contemporary challenges, and conclude with the way ahead and the implications.

Views of Patriotism

Patriotism means different things to different people. Patriotism is usually tied to one's feelings toward their country of origin and polity. Surprisingly, there is much debate over whether patriotism is a virtue or a vice.[1] Early in our nation's history patriotism inspired men like Nathan Hale who in 1776, as he was waiting to be executed, said "I only regret that I have but one life to loose for my country."[2] Abraham Lincoln defined patriotism, specifically American patriotism, as "the devotion not only to country, but also to its principles, in our case, means the principles set down in 1776."[3] Patriotism in its basic form is '"love of country."[4] The true debate is love of country at the expense of what?

Before we go further into the debate, however, let's take a look at the history of the word. "Patriotism" is a relatively new word, but its cognate "patriot" is older and the etymological root, *patria*, is more ancient still.[5] "Patriot" came into early modern English around the sixteenth century and originally referred to a fellow-countryman.[6] In 1688 the "patriot" was tied to a particular set of political principles: defense of liberty and the rights of Englishmen against tyranny.[7] When it made its way across the ocean to the Americas in the 1760's patriotism became the rally cry for the War of Independence. As a young nation we depended on loyalty to the cause and future potential of the fledgling nation. We needed constituents to see beyond their own needs and buy into and accept the ideas of the greater good. A genuine love of the land, the development of a distinct collective identity, and a growing idea of a "conspiracy against liberty"[8] were traits of the patriot. The term represented the politics of the time. It was a call for change and resistance against what were perceived as illegal oppressive rulers.

Over time, as America progressed, people began to challenge what patriotism was. Some began to question it for what they saw as uncritical support of the government... "my country right or wrong" idea.[9] This "uncritical" support has been a contentious issue since the idea of patriotism first came into being. In America the concept that once rallied the country became a point for debate and the debate continues. Throughout history scholars have in fact questioned the virtue of patriotism. In fact, as in the example below from Horatio Smith, some see patriotism as a potential form of discrimination and prejudice that has global implications. There is more on this challenge later in this document but for now I will discuss the opposing views of patriotism a little further.

In ancient times philosophers like Aristotle had opposing views of patriotism. Aristotle refused to rank patriotism among the moral or political virtues in his ethics, and in his politics he went so far as to refrain from ever mentioning even the word for "fatherland" or "country" (patris).[10] Aristotle saw the patriot as one dominated by blind support of the government with little ability for free thinking. Leo Tolstoy saw patriotism as "the principle that will justify the training of wholesale murders."[11] Horatio Smith said, "patriotism, too often the hatred of others countries disguised as the love of one's own."[12] Today the enmity for the idea of patriotism continues. Alasdair MacIntyre says that in its truest form it's the love of one's own country at the expense of others. Patriotism involves a moral judgment that is exclusionary and prejudicial. This judgment leads to conflict.[13]

If patriotism evokes conflict why would we want to foster a nation of patriots? To answer this question we need to understand that patriotism can be defined in many ways, but I will focus on one of the three definitions described in *Patriotism.*[14] Impartial patriotism[15] is the type of parasitism that I feel best describes how Americans view their patriotism.

Impartial patriotism arises from the demands of wider loyalties. It involves support of one's country because it's his and has certain features that appeal to him, but he can also sympathize with other adversaries.[16] This might also be called moderate patriotism. On the other hand, "True" patriotism is described by Alasdair MacIntyre as patriotism that judges based on one's own country's interests with minimal regard for how these interests might conflict or impact on the interests of others.[17]

True patriotism involves the idea that my country is best and every patriot should try to encourage his nation and promote its national interests even if that leads to war.[18] Patriotism conflicts with morality in that expanding wealth involves possession of resources and thus, a willingness to go to war on one's nation's behalf.[19] If patriotism is an absolute faith and allegiance to desires of the government, right or wrong, the potential for negative results would clearly show this idea of patriotism as a vice. However, as is true with most concepts, you have your extremes on the one hand and at some point before you reach the other extreme you can usually find a middle ground. In the case of patriotism the middle ground is moderate patriotism[20].

Most of the opposition against the patriot assumes that they cannot allow for differences of others. In moderate patriotism we assume that one is able to apply moral judgments concerning not only one's own nation, but also the nations of others as well. Those who seek to condemn the patriot fail to account for the potential existence of a universal morality that transcends national ties. There are those that say moderate patriotism is not true patriotism, but is an emasculated form of patriotism.[21] Yet in spite of this, the moderate form is more frequently exercised due to is palatability. It allows for the promotion of one's own interests while applying acceptable judgment that allows one to accept the ways of others. American patriotism has allowed for this moral universality from the beginning and that is why it has endured. If one considers the founding principle that "all men are endowed by nature's god with certain unalienable rights,"[22] a principle embodied in the American Constitution, you can understand that America's ideals naturally allow for "all men."[23]

Patriotism is a challenge for many. The American patriot is continually challenged by those who view patriotism as a vice, yet he is not deterred. By clinging to the principles of liberty and rights for all, American patriotism has not changed and the faithful have remained loyal to the nation throughout our history. I will now take a more in depth look at Patriotism in America.

Patriotism in America

When someone thinks of patriotism and what it means, it might conjure up artifacts such as the American flag, the national anthem, yellow ribbons, men and women in uniform, or even our nation's capitol. All are symbols of America. To remind its citizens of what it has accomplished and the many great Americans who have worked to ensure that the nation lived up to its ideals we have cemented days of recognition into our calendar such as the 4th of July, Veterans Day, Presidents Day, and the Martin Luther King holiday, just to name a few. When you consider the nation's history and what it has accomplished in a relatively short period of time, compared to other nation's in the world, it seems hard to understand how anyone would not feel a swell of patriotic pride. After all, a nations' identity is embodied in the history of its citizens[24] and what Americans have accomplished in just over 200 years is remarkable. We have emerged as the world's hegemonic power and today exercise tremendous influence in the international community. Due to this heritage, Americans have shown their patriotism throughout history and the basis for their patriotism remains unchanged even today. In spite of its consistency, however, it hasn't always been easy. In fact, events in our history have caused the patriot to continually remind themselves what it means to be patriotic in America. This section will focus on patriotism in America, the basic principles on which American patriotism is based, and how those principles have enabled the American patriot to endure.

In 1776, when Nathan Hale was about to be executed by the British, he stated, "I only regret that I have but one life to lose for my country."[25] What was it about America that encouraged such loyalty and devotion? George Washington said, "Citizens by birth or choice, of a common country, that country has a right to concentrate your affections. The name of America which belongs to you, in your national capacity, must always exalt the just pride of Patriotism."[26] In 1852 Abraham Lincoln defined patriotism: American patriotism as "the devotion not only to country, but also to its principles, which, in our case, means the principles set down in 1776.[27] The principles that Lincoln referred to were the principles of liberty and the idea that all men were endowed with certain unalienable rights. These are clearly articulated in the constitution of the United States. It's these principles that have allowed patriotism to endure in America.

Today our national interests drive us to assist the international community in realizing the same principles of liberty and freedom. These principles were the focal point of American patriotism in the 18th century and the ideals have remained at the forefront in motivating the American patriot. With this nation's ongoing efforts to realize its full potential for prosperity and growth and to assist other countries in their quest for liberty and freedom, it has been a challenge for the patriot to remain loyal. The challenges manifest themselves when the ideals on which the patriot bases his patriotism have often been pushed aside. After all, we live in a country that fought a war over slavery, denied certain people the right to vote because of their race and gender, struggled with segregation, is viewed by the international community as a unilateralist nation, and today is being pressured by the idea of tolerance and the influence of moral relativism. These issues can make it hard for the patriot to hold on to those values that inspire the love of country. America, like other nations in the world, is a nation with flaws and these flaws have played out both at home and in the international community. However, remembering the ideals for which it stands and the fact that America is in a continuous struggle to overcome its flaws is what gives hope to the patriot.

In order to understand how this hope has secured the patriots loyalty I will now take a look at the issue of slavery. This was perhaps one of the greatest struggles faced by this country. It split the nation by pitting brother against brother and patriot against patriot. Even today it has impact in the way many African Americans view patriotism. Amazingly both North and South were filled with patriots fighting for the same enduring principles of life and liberty. The difference was that one side felt preservation of the union, so that liberties could be realized for generations to come, was more important than the preservation of one's current way of life. In addition, and perhaps more critical for the purposes of this paper, there was the question concerning the status of African Americans and their right to exercise the same liberties available to other Americans. To truly live up to the ideals of the founding fathers the nation was responsible for ensuring that all Americas were given the same unalienable rights. Continued exclusion would suggest that the founding principles no longer applied and challenge the patriot's basic premise for love of country. Frederick Douglas spoke out against the hypocrisy of America at the time when he spoke of the US as a government that mouthed the language of liberty yet committed "crimes which would disgrace a nation of savages"; of patriotism reduced to "swelling vanity," He was a genuine patriot of dissent.[28] He would also say, "I have no love for America, as such; I have no patriotism. I have no country. What country have I?"[29] His words, though harsh, showed a frustration with the realties of 1847. In spite of these realities, he had great hope and faith in what America could be if the principles were equally applied to all men. It was his hope that enabled him to remain a patriot who sought to force America to live up to what it was intended to be.

Issues over the rights of African Americans continued well into the 1960s and some may argue that they continue today. One author, Roger Wilkins, states that many black Americans find it hard to reconcile the achievement of the founding fathers...and their revulsion at their moral failings with regard to slave holding[30]. Another author, Leroy Davis, states that 'America's blacks have the conscience of America and force it to look in the mirror to perform a reality check[31] ensuring the ideals are never forgotten. In spite of their discontent they remain American citizens, but why. In an article written for *"PHI DELTA KAPPAN"*, an African American teacher, Gloria Landson-Billings, put it best. She writes, "in the 1950's America was flawed, but it was working on being better. And the struggle for racial equality was a clear indicator of its willingness to live up to its promise."[32] Although this was written about actions in the 1950's, America shows this willingness even today and that is what the patriot clings to.

Examples of America's ongoing efforts to continue in her quest to live up to the promise are found in the legislations that resulted from the struggles mentioned earlier. Specifically, the 15th Amendment (1870), the Voting Rights Act (1965), the 19th Amendment of 1920, the case of Brown vs. the Board of Education (1954), and affirmative action laws are all examples of the nation's effort to live up to her promise.

Today the challenges faced by the patriot continue, the current situation in Iraq has resulted in a loss of credibility at home as well as abroad. The question concerning our continued presence in Iraq is one that has yet to be answered to the satisfaction of Americans and our international partners. What has been seen as a primarily unilateral action will continue to degrade US credibility until it is resolved. Kofi Annan spoke of this sentiment in his final address speech in 2006 when he said, "No state can make its own actions legitimate in the eyes of others. When power, especially military force, is used, the world will consider it legitimate only when convinced that it is being used for the right purpose - for broadly shared aims - in accordance with broadly accepted norms." [33] The majority of the international community does not see US involvement in Iraq" as being in accordance with "broadly accepted norms." As a result this struggle will play itself out over the early months of 2007 while the American patriot and the world watch in order to see if the country can again rise to the challenge of its promise of freedom and liberty for all and not just a selected few when it's in our own national interest.

Patriotism in American has faced many challenges and the challenges continue today, but because American strives to live up to the guiding principles upon which American patriotism is founded, the patriot appears able to live through the struggle and accept her with her flaws. The American patriot clings to the hope that the nation will always strive to life up to her promise.

Exercising Patriotism

We have seen how patriotism, rooted in the basic principles laid out in the Constitution, has endured various struggles in America and basically remained unchanged. The way

Americans have exercised their patriotism is what ensures the nations remains on track, continuing the struggle, to overcome her flaws and live up to her guiding principles. Does this mean that the patriot is always active? In this section I will take a look at the consistency with which both the active and passive patriot have exercised their patriotism to ensure the nation lives up to its promise.

In the introduction of the book Patriotism, Igor Primoratz says that patriotism-love of one's country is a love expressed in action...The touchstone of one's patriotism is what one is prepared to do for it.[34] He further states that it requires active participation in interest groups, in public issues, devotion to public causes, and voting.[35] Gloria Landis-Billings indicates that patriots organize, protest, demonstrate, and push for social change. Patriotism is "something that you do, not what you say."[36] Walter Berns[37] suggests that patriotism is a civic duty that requires training. President George W. Bush, in his commencement ceremony to graduates of Ohio State University said,

> Patriotism is expressed by flying the flag, but it is more... America needs more than taxpayers, spectators, and occasional voters. America needs full-time citizens. America needs men and women who respond to the call of duty, who stand up for the weak, who speak up for their beliefs, who sacrifice for a greater good. America needs your energy, and your leadership, and your ambition...[38]

I will discuss how Americans have consistently exercised their patriotism, but first let's consider another patriot that exists in America. This patriot is a passive patriot. It's important to understand the existence of this patriot because if one only looks at the active patriot they might fail to see the full power of patriotism that exists in America. Passive patriotism might seem to contradict the statements above in that it does not necessarily involve an outward display of ongoing action, but it does involve action and should not be considered any less patriotic. Consider the fact that patriotism is an emotional attachment.[39] You can feel emotions without being compelled to act upon them daily. Igor Primoratz was speaking of the passive patriot when he said ..."Americans are wrapped up in their private affairs and they are tolerant of political activists, but generally regard politics as an intrusion."[40] Another author writes that lack of action is the death of patriotism that then withers once its viewed as merely an essential means to the preservation of society for each individual naturally asks, "why should I be the fuel rather than warmed by the fire."[41] The passive patriot may be one who takes time to be "warmed by the fire, but when a meaningful event or issue triggers their need to act they will. The active patriot fuels the fire daily while the passive patriot sits in reserve content with the status quo until a catastrophic event urges them to act. The terrorist attacks of September 11th 2001 are a good example of events that caused even the passive patriot to become active.

Whether temporarily passive or continuously active the American patriot has consistently exercised their patriotism to ensure American lives up to her guiding principles. Patriots upheld the rights of others, by defeating the tyranny of Nazi Germany in World War II. They endured the long standoff during the cold war to ensure that the oppression of communism did not dominate the world. Patriots demonstrated in the 50's and 60's in order to force the nation to end segregation and uphold the rights of all Americans. The expectation was clear and summed up in the words of Martin Luther King when he said, "the nation must deliver on its promise."[42] Patriots were at war in Vietnam while patriots at home protested against the war. Some would question the legitimacy of protesting patriots, but Arthur M. Schlesinger, Jr. refers to Theodore Roosevelt who in 1918 addressed the issue of criticism of the president in wartime. He said that it would be morally treasonable not to criticize the president in wartime because there are traditions in democracy and free discussion and instructive criticism would improve the efficiency of waging of war.[43]

Patriots today continue to protest war as they question the deaths of their fellow compatriots in Iraq who are fighting in a war that's legitimacy is under fire. These same patriots vote to make change. The congressional elections of 2006 were recent example of this. The massive discontent over the administrations actions in Iraq resulted in active patriots changing the balance of power. This has been the patriot's pattern of action throughout our history.

Patriotism is being exercise by the hundreds of thousands of American men and women who choose to voluntarily serve in its Armed Forces. This type of patriotic commitment is the ultimate form of patriotism as describe by Harry Jaffa who says that an active patriot shows a genuine willingness to sacrifice his personal interests, even his very existence. This he says is an absolutely essential fuel for maintaining the fire and the life, of any political society.[44]

America's patriots have shown both support and dissent in the way they have exercised their patriotism. The support is given when the cause has objectives that show America's desire to keeps its promise. Dissent is necessary and essential when the nation deviates from the promise on which the patriots "love of country" is based. This is no truer than today as we dissent over what action to take in order to correct the situation in Iraq. John Kerry, along the lines of Roosevelt said, "at a time like this, those who seek to reclaim America's true character and strength have a duty to speak out and they must be respected."[45]

Regardless of how and when the patriot chooses to demonstrate his patriotism, Abraham Lincoln said, "This country deserves citizens who love and honor it, and are prepared to defend it. We share a birthright to be cared for, improved, and passed on to future generations."[46] The way that Americans have consistently exercised their patriotism shows little change. They continue to demand improvements by voting, serving in the nation's military, serving in civic organizations, demonstrating when necessary, and organizing to push for social change when the nation needs it.

As patriots keep vigilance every day to ensure the country remains focused on living up to its ideals they will continue to face challenges. I will now discuss some of the current challenges on the horizon.

<u>Current Challenges</u>

Patriotism requires conditions that a nation must meet to be suitable to facilitate patriotic loyalty.[47] In the past the US has shown an ongoing desire to live up to the principles set forth in her Constitution and this has facilitated the enduring loyalty of her patriots. However, today we live in a difficult era. As Arthur M. Schlesinger, Jr. said, "it is certainly true that never in American history before has the United States been so unpopular in the world, so distrusted, disliked and even hated."[48] America is not living up to her promise and the American patriot is working harder than ever to maintain his loyalty because the nation's effort to get back on track is questionable and the ongoing situation in Iraq is perhaps the most pressing threat to American patriotism.

The situation in Iraq is contributing to the degradation of world opinion towards the US. Concerning war, Betty Jean Craige writes that the majority of Americans are likely to trust the leaders in the assumption that the leaders know how best to achieve military victory.[49] Iraq has yet to result in what the public perceives as a military victory. When the administration declared an end to the hostilities in Iraq it got another war that it had failed to anticipate. The sectarian violence that followed was not expected and not planned for. One author writes, it was a failure of leadership and only with a public acknowledgment… and long overdue conversation,… why this war… cannot be abandoned without serious consequences,[50] will the US be able to recover from the situation and potentially gain back the national trust it will need to continue in the struggle.

The international reputation of the US is not something to be taken lightly. The interdependence of the world is increasing brought home by globalization. Having a reputation of increasing distrust from the international community will significantly challenge our place in a world where nations are increasingly interdependent. In this environment the idea of making patriots is complicated. American patriotism is now subject to scrutiny more than ever and some may be drawn away from the idea entirely, as the bond uniting people moves away from their country and what it represents to a bond of common interests that now crosses international borders due to advances in technology that have resulted in globalization.

Betty Jean Craige discusses what she believes will lead to success in a global society in her book, *American Patriotism in a Global Society.* She says that it will depend on the degree to which a society subordinates its individual cultural or national interests to transcultural and transnational laws and institutions.[51] It will also demand allegiance to laws vice an allegiance to men because they engender profoundly different political values. Whereas allegiance to men produces relationships of opposition to groups perceived to be alien, allegiance to law allows for cooperation between the group and other groups in the world, even group's historically enemies. This creates harmonious interaction in a global society.[52] For Americans, currently the only dominant world power, this subordination is a new concept.

American patriotism depends on a unique set of ideals and characteristics that originate from American culture and history. Craige suggest that for Americans to survive in a global society they must subordinate this heritage and this will require a paradigm shift. If however, you consider again the basic principles from which American patriotism originates it should allow, when properly applied, for being a good neighbor,[53] which is a mandatory trait for successful participation in a global society.

Additional challenges come from the idea of tolerance and multiculturalism. Since the 1980's schools have adopted teaching a multi-ethnic and polyglot concepts which is more in line with an increasingly interrelated world.[54] Children are educated in multiculturalism and tolerance which under cuts love of country.[55] Walter Berns sees tolerance as a threat to patriotism in that it discourages the patriot from loving those traits he feels are admirable about his own country because tolerance implies that no country is better than another. Multiculturalism is a threat to patriotism in that it emphasizes maintaining ones cultural identity over any national loyalty. It gives higher priority to cultural and ideological pluralism than to a national unity. Multiculturalism supports cultures maintaining their identity in a larger society that desires to consume them.[56] It resists integration which seeks to produce a cultural amalgamation (national unity), which requires the submergence of a supposed original ethnic identity in a new, evolving culture.[57] As these cultural groups develop their ties extend beyond the boundaries of America and reach to those who share like cultural identities. The threat is that this will potentially diminish their desire or need to be part of the greater American identity. It is essentially a "systematic dismantling of America's unitary national identity."[58] It is a country's national identity that produces 'love of country" and forms the basis for patriotism.

These challenges are no less daunting than the challenges the patriot has faced in the past.

Implications and the Way Ahead

Walter Berns says that "making of patriots cannot be left to chance it must be cultivated."[59] This is a responsibility the US cannot take lightly. We cannot bully people into patriotism. The nation must inspire it though action which then results in reciprocal patriotic involvement from it citizens. In the aftermath of September 11th, 2001 people were hungry for rituals. The new wave of orchestrated patriotism was aimed at closing down debate and dissent through prescribed allegiance.[60] We cannot close down the debate, especially over military action that stems from patriotic dissent. In fact, it goes against basic American liberties. Eric Foner writes, "the most patriotic act of all is the unyielding defense of civil liberties, the right to dissent and equality before the law for all Americans.[61] If we discourage dissent we risk runaway policies that will further alienate us from the international community and weaken our role as an international super power. Dissent is the way to demand change. In Iraq it will be the role of the dissenting patriot to move the nation towards a time when governments will have to work to justify, with greater clarity, their desire to risk the lives of their countrymen.[62]

How then does the patriot deal with multiculturalism, tolerance, and the expectations of a global society? Steady state moderate patriotism is the key. Today more than ever the American patriots must show a greater acceptance of others while promoting their own interests. America must keep its tendency of egocentric behavior in check and realize that the American way of doing things may not be exactly transportable to the international community who seek similar rights and freedoms. America's moderate patriots still rooted in the principles of liberty and the attainment of unalienable rights for all, can persevere in this challenging world of increasing globalization. They must simply promote the interests of country while applying moral rules that apply universally,[63] this has been and must continue to be the American patriots enduring legacy.

Conclusion

With the current complexities of the world some suggest that American patriotism is changing. In fact, as this paper has explained, patriotism in American is not changing.

America is a nation of moderate patriots. This has enabled patriots to actively move the nation forward while understanding and supporting the rights of others. This idea is firmly rooted in our Constitution which seeks to promote the basic principles of liberty and the entitlement of unalienable rights for all. Holding firm to these principles American patriotism has endured, unchanging, in spite of external criticism and numerous internal struggles that exposed the nation's flaws.

Whether an active patriot, involved in daily struggles, or a passive patriot, whose action is spurned by certain events like the terrorist attacks of September 11th 2001, the patriot has actively pursued patriotism through demonstrating, voting, protesting, dissent, organizing, and voluntary support of civic organizations. This has not changed.

Today the patriot continues to face challenges. They are dealing with an increasingly deteriorating international opinion and the suggestion that society will require subordination of one's patriotic love of country, usually based on enduring principles seen as better than those demonstrated by other nations, in order to ensure success in a global society. Another challenge comes in dealing with failed policy. One author writes that we risk loosing our patriots if we have brought to question, to much, the qualities we have demonstrated in our policies.[64] Clearly our demonstrated policies, especially the policy surrounding our operations in Iraq need to be addressed in order to turn the tide of international mistrust and to maintain the loyalty of the patriot. The patriot must see more proof of the struggle to right the wrongs if they are to remain loyal.

In overcoming the challenge the moderate patriotism exercised by the majority of Americans must continue to allow for the rights of others. Appling our constitutional principles, of the rights to liberty and freedom, to the international community will allow American patriotism to endure, as it always has, unchanging in spite of the call to subordination. In addition, the support of the dissenting patriot will keep the nation diligent in upholding the principles on which she was founded. We cannot afford to let failed policy continue to foster the degradation in international public opinion towards the US. In addition, we cannot risk the potential for isolation in a world that is thriving on globalization. Our prosperity and power are on the line.

If our patriots can continue to hold firm to the principles of liberty and unalienable rights for all, then they can continue to love their country and accept that others deserve the right to be different. They must force the nation to move away from unilateral action that seems to rely more on the military than any other instrument of power and increasingly seek to engage in politics through more diplomatic means. This will allow us to achieve our own national interests without alienating the international community.

Endnotes

[1] Igor Primoratz, ed., *Patriotism* (Amherst, New York: Humanity Books, 2002), 102.

[2] Walter Berns, *Making Patriots* (Chicago, IL: University of Chicago Press, 2001), 1.

[3] Ibid., 82.

[4] Primoratz, 10.

[5] Ibid., 202.

[6] Ibid., 204.

[7] Ibid., 205.

[8] Ibid., 208.

[9] Ibid., 210.

[10] Harry Jaffa, "Patriotism; American Style-Includes an article on a reply to Thomas Pangles' Patriotism," *National Review* (29 November 1985): [Journal on-line]; available from htt;://findarticles.com/p/articles/mi_m1282/is_v37/ai_4036183; Internet; accessed 14 September 2006.

[11] Primoratz, 60.

[12] Ibid.

[13] Ibid., 12.

[14] Ibid, *Patriotism* is a compilation of papers from various prestigious University Professors throughout the US. Representing backgrounds in philosophy, political science, and social science they discuss the wide ranging debate concerning patriotism.

[15] Ibid., 33.

[16] Ibid., 34.

[17] Ibid., 62.

[18] Ibid., 36.

[19] Ibid., 46, MacIntyre says that true patriotism excludes all other forms of patriotism such as "moderate patriotism" which he sees as emasculated. He allows for no compromise of "true" patriotism.

[20] Ibid., 88, Moderate Patriots are those who are loyal to their country but also upholding to a universal morality.

[21] Ibid., 46.

[22] Berns, 9.

[23] Ibid., 8.

[24] Betty Jean Craige, *American Patriotism In a Global Society* (Albany, New York: State University of New York Press, 1996), 35.

[25] Berns, 1.

[26] Primoratz, 201.

[27] Berms, 82.

[28] Eric Forner, "True Patriotism," *The Nation* (July 2004) [Journal on-line]; available from http://www.findarticles.com; Internet: accessed 14 September 2006.

[29] Berns, 104.

[30] Mark Goldblatt, "America's Black History: Reconciling Patriotism with Slavery's Legacy." *Reason* (April 2002); available from http://www.findarticles.com; Internet; accessed 14 September 2006. Goldblatt reviews: Jefferson's Pillow: The Founding Fathers and the Dilemma of Black Patriotism, by Roger Wilkins.

[31] Leroy Davis, "Digging in America's Backyard: Southern artist Omar Thompson questions notions of patriotism-protest & art," *Colorlines Magazine: Race, Action, Culture* (Fall 2003): available from http://www.findarticles.com/p/articles/mi_m0KAY/is_3_6/ai_108693826; Internet; accessed 14 September 2006.

[32] Gloria Landson-Billings, "Once Upon a Time When Patriotism Was not What You Did," *Phi Delta Kappan* (April 2006): 586 [Journal on-line]; available from http://www.findarticles.com; Internet; accessed 14 September 2006.

[33] Kofi Annan speech on BBC Website, www//news.bbc.co.uk/2/hi/americas/6170089.stm; Accessed 26 December 2006.

[34] Primoratz., 10.

[35] Ibid., 265.

[36] Landson-Billings., 588.

[37] Berns., 65.

[38] President Bush's Commencement Speech to Ohio State University Graduates, Columbus Ohio, website, www.whitehouse.gov/news/releases/2002/06/200020614-1.html, accessed 31 DEC 06.

[39] John Bodnar, ed., *Bonds of Affection, Americans Define their Patriotism* (Princeton, New Jersey: Princeton University Press, 1996), 21, Bodnar states…patriotism is an active emotional attachment born of early training and affinities.

[40] Primoratz., 267.

[41] Harry Jaffa, "Patriotism: American Style-Includes an article on a reply to Thomas Pangles' Patriotism," *National Review* (29 November 1985): [Journal on-line]; available from

htt;://findarticles.com/p/articles/mi_m1282/is_v37/ai_4036183; Internet; accessed 14 September 2006.

[42] Bodar., 1.

[43] Arthur M. Schlesinger Jr., *Books: War and the American Presidency*, website, Washingtonpost.com; Internet; accessed 31 December 2006.

[44]Harry Jaffa, "Patriotism; American Style-Includes an article on a reply to Thomas Pangles' Patriotism," *National Review* (29 November 1985): [Journal on-line]; available from htt;://findarticles.com/p/articles/mi_m1282/is_v37/ai_4036183; Internet; accessed 14 September 2006.

[45] John Kerry, "Patriotism Means Telling the Truth, Making America Stronger," May 6 2006, linked from (*John Kerry Home Page*), available at http://www.johnkerry.com; Internet; accessed 31 December 2006.

[46] Berns., xi.

[47] Primoratz., 102.

[48] Schlesinger.

[49] Craige., 31.

[50] Joe Klein, "The Danger of Yellow Ribbon Patriotism", *TIME, Web Exclusive* (23 August 2005) |www.time.com/time/columnist/klein/article/0,9565,1096435-2,00.html, accessed 1 Jan 07.

[51] Craige., 42.

[52] Ibid., 30.

[53] Ibid., 120. Craige says that today's patriot will best serve the nation by motivating the nation to be a good neighbor in a community of nations.

[54] Phil Scranton, ed., *Beyond September 11th, An Anthology of Dissent* (Archway Rd, London: Pluto Press, 2002), 176.

[55] Mary Walsh, "What Happened to Patriotism?" *Human Events* (21 May 2001): [journal on-line]; available from http://www.findarticles.com; Internet; accessed 14 September 2006.

[56] Betty Jean Craige, *American Patriotism In a Global Society* (Albany, New York: State University of New York Press, 1996), 63.

[57] Ibid., 64.

[58] Ibid.

[59] Ibid., 11.

[60] Scranton., 173.

[61] Scranton., 176.

[62] Ibid.

[63] Primoratz., 102.

[64] Ibid.

End